Him:

'How is it, now you're forty, you don't scream when you climax?'

Her:

'I do, but you're never there.'

△ ◁ ▷ △

Feeling old and depressed because you're forty?

Cheer up! It could be worse; you could be pregnant!

When you turn forty your sex life is a bit like Elvis – it may still be alive but nobody knows for sure.

△ ◁ ▷ ◁

When you're forty you may have difficulty holding on to your youth.

One solution is to try giving him money.

You go through three stages of sex in life: exciting sex, necessary sex and hallway sex. You have exciting sex in your twenties – that's when you and your partner can't keep your hands off each other and do it constantly, at any time and in any position. You have necessary sex in your thirties – you and your partner do it out of a sense of obligation, more as a set routine than with any great passion. Then, in your forties, you have hallway sex – that's when you and your partner pass each other in the hallway and scream: 'Screw you . . .'

'Yeah, screw you too!'

△▽

Him:

'I think at your age you should be looking after your health a bit more. Do you really think you should have a cigarette after we've had sex?'

Her:

'You're probably right – one drag a night is enough!'

△▽▷△

Callow youth:

'I've never slept with a woman over forty before. Do you mind if I ask: are you asthmatic?'

Older woman:

'No – I was hissing your performance!'

△ ▽

The secret of staying young
is to take plenty of exercise,
eat the right food and
lie about your age.

△ ▽ ▷ △

A woman in her forties is
all wised up about men. She
knows that when she's on top
sex is always better because
men always screw up!

▷◁

When I was forty I found a grey pubic hair. When I told my friend she said: 'I knew you hadn't been getting much but don't let it worry you such a lot!'

△▽▷△

If you're over forty, the telephone numbers in your little black book are not girls', but doctors'.

Many of my forty-year-old friends are divorced. They're always moaning about the alimony they are paying – the screwing she gives for the screwing he got.

You know you're over forty by what's on your bedside table. Where there was once condoms and the *Karma Sutra* there's now Night Nurse and sleeping tablets.

Now you're forty why not lose fourteen stone of fat?
Divorce him!

When you're forty you'll find that if you help a man he'll always come back to you . . . when he next wants you to do something for him.

△ ◁

When you're forty you can do without a man altogether. You've got a parrot who swears, a cat who stays out all night, a dog who snores and you're getting screwed by the Inland Revenue.

When you're over forty and a fella asks you to go for a dirty weekend, he may say:

'Let's pretend we're a married couple.'

Be warned: chances are, when he gets into bed he'll turn over, scratch his balls and go to sleep.

△ ◁

At forty you'll know what Yuppie stands for:

Young Useless Prat Probably Incapable of Erection.

△ ◁ ▷ △

When you're forty and a fella making love to you says he thinks you must be a virgin – you've still got your tights on.

If you meet a fella who
likes virgins – knot your pubic
hairs together: he'll not know
the difference and the pain's the
same.

If you call a man of forty your
baby he's probably
bald, toothless and covered
in snot.

△◁

Conversation for the over forties:

Her (on noticing the guy's left his flies undone and trying to be helpful):

'Excuse me but I think your garage door is undone.'

Him *(trying to be macho)*:

'Really? And how did you like the Rolls-Royce you saw there?'

Her *(crushingly)*:

'I didn't see any Rolls – just a mini with two flat tyres.'

▷◁

Forty-year-old man after having made love:

'Am I your first?'

Woman:

'You may be.
You look familiar.'

△ ◁

Over forty you no longer mind your gynaecologist putting in two fingers. In fact you insist on a second opinion.

Men over forty who you used to think dreamboats now look like tugboats – and the jetty's collapsed.

How do forty-year-olds hold their liquor?

By the ears!

△ ▽ ▷ ◁

You may feel a bit more daring about sex when you're over forty but if your partner fantasises about getting you to join him in bed with another woman, say you'd be delighted to have someone to talk with when he falls asleep as usual five minutes after getting into bed.

And if he offers to give you something you haven't had before reply:

'Satisfaction?'

△ ◁

My friend was forty the other day and her toyboy gave her a great present.

He said:

'I'm going to kiss your bellybutton.'

'Big deal!' she said, 'I've had that done hundreds of times.'

He said:

'What? From the *inside*?'

A friend of mine – over forty – said to me:

'I don't mind having a test-tube baby provided it's a nine-inch test tube.'

We've all got different tastes in men, I know, but I can't understand what my friend sees in her bald, fat, forty-year-old partner who keeps on licking his eyebrows with his tongue.

Now I'm over forty those Aids posters annoy me – I mean the ones which say: 'Is ten minutes of pleasure worth a lifetime of regret?'

They would be much more useful if they told my partner how to give me ten minutes of pleasure!

I have to confess, now I'm over forty I sometimes get a bit sex-starved. The other day I was walking round B & Q when an assistant offered me a screw for my doorknob.

I said:

'Sure, and I'll throw in a toaster.'

Now I'm over forty, when the hunky aerobics instructor says:

'I'm going to lick you women into shape,' I give a cheer.

△ ◁ ▷ △

When you're over forty, you need a man who's well-informed – in other words, someone who agrees with you.

Now you're over forty you've decided you learn by your mistakes – and no-one has had a better education than you.

△ ▽ ▷ ◁

Why do women drive more slowly than men?

Because they'll do anything to stay under forty.

Why do most over-forties prefer sex to playing bowls?

The balls are lighter and they don't have to change their shoes.

Now my fella's over forty I'm getting rid of him. I'm fed up with the way he treats my body like a temple – somewhere to visit on Sundays. Apparently his bimbo secretary said she would do anything for a fur coat and now she can't do it up.

Two women in their forties having a conversation:

First woman:

'I keep reading that too much sex is bad for you, so I'm giving it up.'

Second woman *(surprised)*:

'What, sex?'

First woman:

'No, reading!'

Now I'm over forty I've started going to church. I have to admit it is quite fun. Last week the vicar let me choose the three hymns.

I said:

'I'll have him, him and him . . .'

Undertaker:

'Would you like your husband buried or cremated?'

Widow:

'Why take chances – let's do both!'

My friend says now she's over forty she gets more fellas than ever. Young girls don't like men who kiss and tell but she welcomes all the advertising she can get. She says she now has what they all like: a clean body and a dirty mind.

Now she's in her forties my friend has to be very careful with her health. She tells me she has a very rare medical condition: when she sneezes she has an orgasm.

I asked her what she was taking for it and she said:

'Pepper!'

A beauty tip for women in their forties who have large breasts. Get rid of your bras and your face will look years younger. The weight pulls all the wrinkles out.

Men in their forties may notice that that part of their anatomy which once stood up in the mornings and watched them shave, now hangs down sadly and watches them shine their shoes.

Men in their forties may find that what they once stayed up all night doing now takes them all night to do once. Still, they can play gambling games to pass the time: once they finally get it up they can bet on which way it's going to fall.

My girlfriend complained that now I was over forty my organ was getting smaller.

I said:

'It wasn't any smaller, just not used to playing in a cathedral.'

She said:

'It was more like putting a marshmallow in a money-box.'

Men over forty may have to pace themselves a little more when they're making love. A friend of mine found an ideal way to pace himself on Sunday morning, which was when he usually liked to have sex. He would keep time with the church bells as they rang ding, dong, ding, dong . . . He would still be alive now if that fire engine hadn't gone by . . .

For a woman over forty, a husband is often like a grumbling appendix – there's a lot of pain having it removed but you'll find you didn't need it.

Women in their forties mature like good wine – they become full-bodied and voluptuous. Men on the other hand are like old cheese – they just get smelly and eventually you have to throw them out.

When you're over forty one way to improve your sex life is to have separate beds. My friend says her sex life has never been so good since she and her husband got separate beds. Her bed is in London, his is in New York.

△ ◁

Woman trying to comfort grieving friend: 'You'll never find a husband like him again.'

Widow:

'I certainly don't intend to take the chance!'

There's one difference in sexual behaviour between men and women over forty – men like to have the light on when they have sex, women like to have the light off – a man likes to see what he's getting, a woman knows what she's getting and would rather not see it!

A friend of mine says now her husband's over forty he tends to come too quickly. However, she's found a way of slowing him down. Just as he is approaching climax she whispers in his ear:

'Oh darling, I forgot to tell you, the Inland Revenue phoned today, but don't worry, I hung up on him.'

If you're over forty and don't like using the pill or condoms, try Vaseline as a contraceptive. Send your partner to the bathroom to get you a glass of water. Before he comes back, smear the door knob to the bedroom with Vaseline and close the door firmly – that way he'll never get back in again!

When you're over forty a man may need to be a little less than subtle in signalling his needs. At Christmas, for instance, try pinning the mistletoe to your trousers.

Now she's forty my friend's quite picky – she treats penises like fish: the small ones she throws back, the big ones she mounts.

△ ◁

Doctor:

'Now you're forty, how often do you have sex?'

Woman:

'Infrequently.'

Doctor:

'Is that two words?'

Some women in their forties turn to food as a substitute for sex. If they're really kinky they put a mirror over the dining-room table!

△ ▽ ▷ ◁

A forty-year old friend of mine got charged with indecent exposure for taking off all his clothes on the beach but was acquitted for lack of evidence.

Love, companionship and sex are what a woman needs from a man. By the time a woman reaches forty she knows she will have to go to three different addresses.

△ ▽ ▷ ◁

△ ▽ ▷ ◁

Forty-year-old woman:

'Do you know, for twenty years my husband and I were perfectly happy.'

Her friend:

'So, what went wrong?'

Forty-year-old woman:

'We met!'

Forty-year-old woman complaining about the decline of morals:

'I never had sex with my husband before we were married. Did you?'

Second woman:

'I might have done. What's his name?'

△ ▽ ▷ △

Women over forty prefer the strong silent type of man. He doesn't interrupt when she's talking.

△ ▽

Forty-year-old women only marry for love provided he's got lots of money.

What drives most women of forty-plus nuts is when their partners forget their birthday but remember their age.

Men over forty often take up fishing as it is the only opportunity they have for hearing someone say:
'Wow, that's a big one!'

△ ▽

First woman:

'If your husband's such a bad lover I'm surprised you still sleep with him.'

Second woman:

'Oh well, he's better than yours.'

A vet called his forty-five-year-old receptionist, Mrs Jones, in to his surgery where he was doing a post mortem on a dead horse.

'Mrs Jones,' he said, 'look at the size of that horse's equipment! Have you ever seen anything like it?'

'Well,' Mrs Jones replied, 'it reminds me a bit of my husband's.'

'What, the size of it?' said the vet much impressed.

'No,' she said, 'but it's got about as much life in it!'

It's the morning of Christmas Eve and a woman, a little over forty, says to her husband:

'Darling, shall I give the milkman a Christmas tip?'

'No,' said her husband, 'give him a mince pie and screw him.'

When he came back from work he was horrified to find his wife in bed with the milkman.

'What on earth are you doing?' he demanded.

'Exactly what you told me to do!' she replied.

Men can be classified into three sexually active age groups:

Men in their twenties
– **tri-weekly**

Men in their thirties
– **try weekly**

Men in their forties
– **try weakly**

△ ◁

At forty most women know better than to date a man who drives a Porsche. Generally he makes love like he drives: he goes too fast, gets there before anyone else, and stops suddenly.

▷◁

A fella in his late forties went to his doctor and said:

'Doc, can you lower my sex drive?'

The doctor said:

'Are you sure this sex drive isn't just in your head?'

'Yes,' the fella answered, 'that's just the problem: you've got to lower it a little!'

△ ◁ ▷ ◁

A fella of fifty went to the doctor and said:

'Doctor, please examine me to see if I'm sexually fit.'

The doctor said:

'Certainly, show me your sex organs.'

With that the fella put out his tongue and lifted his index finger.

Age is an awful thing. When you were a girl you used to buy KY Jelly; now you use Polygrip!

△ ◁

Time may be a great healer but it's no beauty specialist.

△ ◁ ▷ ◁

△ ▽

If you're over forty and still single, the chances are you've looked at the personal ads in the hope of meeting some attractive men. What follows are some hints on reading between the lines:

Man looking for a satisfying relationship **(He wants sex)**

Man wants discreet companionship **(He wants sex and he's married)**

Man loves opera **(He wants sex and he's been to the opera once)**

Responsible male **(He wants sex and has a job)**

By the time a woman celebrates her fortieth birthday she should have three types of animal in her life:

A mink on her back,

a jaguar in her garage,

and a tiger in her bed.

A woman over forty likes a man with a will of his own – made out in her favour.

△ ◁ ▷ ◁

Women over forty have learnt that contraceptives should be used on every *conceivable* occasion.

Women of forty are smart: when they get a diaphragm fitted, they make sure it comes with a service contract!

△ ◁ ▷ △

Women of forty know men are like public toilets – engaged or full of shit.

'Now he's forty, does your husband still look at younger women?'

'Yes, but he can't remember why.'

△ ▽ ▷ △

'An archaeologist is the best husband a woman can have.'

'Why do you say that?'

'The older she gets, the more interested he is in her.'

'I found my husband dead in bed.'

'How did you know he was dead?'

'He was stiff for more than two minutes.'

Women over forty know the secret of eternal youth – they lie about their age.

The forty-year-old woman longs to have children.

The forty-year-old man longs to date them.

When men over forty start using hairspray, enjoy it. Their hair is normally the stiffest thing about them.

△ ▽

Glenda Jackson at forty eight:

'The important thing in acting is to be able to laugh or cry. If I have to cry I think of my sex life. If I have to laugh I think of my sex life.'

A forty-nine-year-old guy staring mournfully at his prick said:

'We were born together, we grew up together, we got married together – why, oh why, did you have to die before me.'

Woody Allen at forty nine:

'Don't knock masturbation – it's sex with someone you love.

△ ▽ ▷ ◁

Rodney Dangerfield at forty nine:

'If it weren't for pickpockets I'd have no sex life at all.'

Jean Harlow:

'I like to wake up every morning feeling a new man.'

△ ▽ ▷ △

Gypsy Rose Lee:

'I have everything I had twenty years ago – except now it's all lower.

Christian Dior:

'Women are the most fascinating between the ages of thirty five and forty, after they have won a few races and know how to pace themselves. Since few women ever pass forty, maximum fascination can continue indefinitely.'

▷◁

Inside every young, slim, girl, there is a fat middle-aged woman waiting to get out.

△ ◁ ▷ △

Most forty-year-old women have found out that marriage involves three rings: an engagement ring, a wedding ring, and suffering.

Most unmarried women over forty know that all attractive men have one thing in common: they're married.

The only way I can get my husband to do push-ups now he's forty is to put the TV remote control between his toes.

When I was twenty, getting ready to go out on a date took no time at all. Now at forty it takes two hours. If I live to be eighty, it'll take so long to get ready, I'll never go out at all.

△ ◁

A woman in her forties was trying on hats in a department store. Just as she put a very expensive hat on her head, an extremely smooth salesman sidled up and said:

'Wow, madam looks at least ten years younger in that hat.'

'Then I definitely won't have it,' snapped the woman.

Baffled, he said

'Why not?'

'Well,' she said, 'I don't want to look ten years older every time I take it off, now do I?'

▷◁

My friend at forty showed a real sense of style. She put in a gold diaphragm so that her fella could come into the money!

△ ◁ ▷ △

You're over the hill at forty when you feel like the morning after when you could swear you haven't been anywhere.

'Do you know, my husband celebrated his midlife crisis by running off with the au-pair.'

'Oh, how awful for you.'

'Yes, now I've got to do the ironing myself!'

In your forties the best thing to exercise is discretion.

▷◁

Now you're forty, you know that sex is only dirty when it's done right.

△ ◁ ▷ △

Forty is the old age of youth, fifty is the youth of old age.

When a man reaches forty without marrying, he probably never will. He'll never find someone who loves him more than he does.

Women of forty are at their best but men at forty are too stupid to realise it.

Few women of forty admit their age: few men of forty act theirs.

At twenty we don't care what the world thinks of us.

At thirty we worry what the world thinks of us.

At forty we realise the world isn't thinking of us at all.

Women in their forties speak frankly about sex. When my friend tried to talk to her husband about mutual orgasm, he thought she was talking about an insurance company.

By the time you reach your forties you know never to take anyone to bed in the afternoon. Someone better is bound to come along later.

△▽

It's not just life which begins at forty; also hot flushes, bad eyesight, arthritis, and driving everyone mad by telling them the same stories over and over again.

△▽▷△

You know you're forty when you start turning the lights out for economic rather than romantic reasons.

Women of forty are smart: they know the difference between gifts and guilt gifts. Guilt gifts are better.

For women over forty diamonds are a girl's best friend. For a man over forty a dog is often his best friend which is why they call man a dumb animal.

Men age badly: first they forget names, then they forget faces, then they forget to pull their zipper up and finally they forget to pull their zipper down!

Women in their forties sometimes take up jogging – just so that they can hear heavy breathing again.

They say at forty you're as young as you feel. Depressing isn't it.

△ ◁

Being forty means that when a man says he wants to be alone with you, you're worried that his motives might be pure.

▷ △

Forty is when you think all your friends are beginning to show their age. Fifty is when you realise it's not just your friends who are showing their age.

My friend says her husband has everything Tom Cruise has except youth, money, charm and looks!

▷◁

Forty is:

1. When you can't believe how bad pop groups have become and people laugh when you talk about your 'record' collection.

2. When *you* need alteration – not your clothes.

3. When your medicine cabinet is better stocked than your drinks cabinet.

△▽

A friend of mine went to the doctor complaining of feeling tired all the time. When the doctor heard he was forty he said:

'You are suffering from a deficiency.'

'But I take every vitamin under the sun,' my friend wailed.

'I'm afraid the deficiency you suffer from,' said the doctor, 'is youth deficiency!'

When unmarried men reach forty they address their love letters 'to whom it may concern'!

The doctor told my friend when she was forty that she was as fit as a twenty year old internally. It was just externally she looked worn out.

△ ◁

Nothing makes a woman feel her age more than her younger lover being bald.

△ ◁ ▷ ◁

Why do women have the change of life in their forties? To give men-a-pause!

Men in their forties can be inconsiderate. My friend gave his wife an airpistol for Christmas. She was so pissed off she bought him a T-shirt with a target on it.

You know you are in your forties when you try to straighten out the wrinkles in your tights and then find you aren't wearing any.

For most men in their forties, the gleam in their eye is caused by the light hitting their glasses!

When a woman in her forties wants to stop a man harassing her she doesn't say:

'Leave me alone!'

She says:

'I love you. I want to marry you and have your children.'

△ ◁ ▷ △

A friend of mine bumped into a glamorous forty-year-old woman in the hotel lobby.

He said:

'If the rest of you is as soft as your bosom, you'll forgive me.'

She said:

'If the rest of you is as hard as your elbow I am in room 205.'

This couple had been married fifteen years. The husband said:

'Our sex life is so boring. Why don't we try some different positions?'

She said:

'All right – you stand behind the ironing board and I'll lie on the sofa farting.'

△ ◁

A woman of forty saw a sign in a pet shop she felt she had to investigate. It read:

Clitoris-licking frog inside.

She went into the shop and before she could open her mouth the man behind the counter said:

'Bonjour Madame . . .'

▷◁

A woman in her forties was working in a publishing house. She was helping compile a new edition of a dictionary. When she came to the word 'small' she thought for a moment and changed the definition to:

'Is it in yet?'

What does a man in his forties have in his pants which a woman in her forties has on her face?

Wrinkles.

Women in their forties know that a man is like a snow storm: you never know when he's coming, how many inches you'll get or how long he'll stay.

Ask a woman in her forties the difference between 'ooh' and 'ahhh' - she'll tell you about three inches!

△ ◁ ▷ △

Ask any woman in her forties what comes after 69 and she'll answer:

Listerine!

A man had been married fifteen years and his wife had always beaten him at everything from tennis to sex. He racked his brains trying to think of something he could beat her at. At last he had an idea. He said to her:

> 'Let's pee against the garden wall and whoever pees the highest wins the game.'

'OK.', said his wife and, without hesitation, went to the wall lifted up her dress, then her leg and peed about six inches above the ground.

Eager to prove his superiority her husband unzipped his fly, pulled out his penis and was just about to pee when his wife interrupted.

'Come on,' she said. 'No cheating. No hands allowed!'

Ask any man the difference between anxiety and panic and he'll say: 'Anxiety is the first time you can't do it. Panic is the second time you can't do it the first time!'

Women in their forties are very smart. They know that pillows are designed to be put under the arse, not the head!

Women over forty invented the most effective method of birth control: laughter.

Women over forty know that the reason they have a pussy is so that men will talk to them!

Women in their forties prefer hunters as lovers. They go deep into the bush, always shoot twice, and always eat what they shoot.

△ ▽ ▷ △

Women in their forties know that God gave them nipples to make suckers out of men.

My ecologically-minded friend has invented the first organic vibrator — by crossing a Mexican jumping bean with a cucumber.

△ ▽ ▷ △

Women in their forties know the difference between a clitoris and a pub — men can always find a pub.

△ ◁

A woman in her forties was having trouble with her sex life so she went to a marriage guidance counsellor for advice. She explained to the counsellor:

'Every time my husband climaxes he lets out an ear-shattering scream.'

'Well,' said the counsellor, 'doesn't that give you just a little bit of satisfaction?'

'No!' replied the woman, 'I'm just pissed off at being woken up!'

▷◁

Women in their forties know the difference between worry and panic: about twenty eight days.

▷◁

Women in their forties know the four biggest lies told by men are:

'Of course I love you',
'The cheque's in the post',
'I promise I won't come in your mouth', **and**
'Honestly, it's only a cold sore.'

Women in their forties often take up playing bridge because bridge is like sex – if you've got a good hand you don't need a partner.

After years of studying men, women in their forties know what hats and haemorrhoids have in common – sooner or later every arsehole gets one!

Two women in their forties are talking,

First woman:
'How's your husband nowadays?'

Second woman:
'He died.'

First woman:
'I am sorry. I didn't know. What did he die of?'

Second woman:
'V.D.'

First woman:
'But you don't die of V.D. in this day and age!'

Second woman:
'You bloody do if you give it to me!'

△ ▽ ▷ ◁

A woman in her forties was proudly showing off her mink coat to her friend who said to her:

'Aren't you ashamed when you think of the poor dumb beast who suffered so much so you could have that coat?'

The first woman just shrugged and said:

'Listen, my husband deserves all the suffering he gets!'

Women in their forties know a lot about financial matters. For instance she'll tell you there is no such thing as a wife over-drawing her husband's account – it's just a case of the husband under-depositing it!

△ ▽ ▷ ◁

My friend was being seduced by a young stud. He said, after the first sexual encounter: 'I want to make love to you in the worst possible way!' She said: 'You just have.'

△ ▽ ▷ ◁

My friend who's been married fifteen years calls sex with her husband 'Trivial Pursuit'.

If in your forties you aren't getting enough sex you can't help reading sex into anything which is said to you. For example, the **doctor says**:

'Take your clothes off';

the **dentist says**:

'Open wide';

the **hairdresser says**:

'Do you want it teased or blown?';

the **banker says**:

'If you take it out you'll lose interest';

and the **interior decorator says**:

'You'll like it when it's in'.

Men in their forties can have real sexual problems. A friend of mine who suffered from premature ejaculation went to a counselling meeting but no-one was there. He was two hours early!

Women like men in their forties to keep fit. Unfortunately they often find the only time their man wakes up stiff is when he has been overdoing it in the gym the day before.

Most women over forty have discovered that the best way to stop a man from wanting to have sex is to marry him.